HIGH OCTANE PERFORMANCE

Getting Focused On What Matters Most!

BY

CLARENCE WILLIAMS

EDITED BY SARAH CHOY

Get a FREE High Octane Performance Worksheet at
http://highoctaneperformance.com/worksheet

Published by: Push Button Publishing
Push Button Local Marketing, LLC
11877 DOUGLAS RD STE 102
JOHNS CREEK, GA 30005
PB-PUBLISHING.COM

DEDICATION

To my children - I expect you to read this in your teenage years. The exercises in this book are the things I would like for you to do before you leave home as an adult and decide to go out on your own. I believe you were born to be members of a talented 10 percent of society that is responsible for making contributions that will shape the future.

CONTENTS

ACKNOWLEDGMENTS

I am grateful to the hundreds of unnamed people that I've shared this concept with over the past twenty years. Your continuous feedback is what sparked the development and completion of this book.

There are so many seemingly unrecognized contributions from friends and family that make writing a book possible. Thanks to all of the people who make up my relationship wheel. Your love is part of the fuel that makes up the successes I've experienced so far in my life.

WHY THIS BOOK IS IMPORTANT

May you live in interesting times.
—Chinese proverb

When I was in my early twenties, I was working in the telecommunications industry selling cellular phones. At that time, it seemed like every year new communications technologies were being introduced; we were at the beginning stages of a new era. It was before the introduction and mass distribution of smartphones or what we now call personal digital assistants (PDAs). I was just out of college and it was the early 1990s, a few years before the 1996 Telecommunications Act and the tremendous growth of the information superhighway. At that time, having a cellular phone was a luxury and in some ways served as a status symbol. If you carried one of those big bulky telephones without wires, it sent a message that you were important—or at least that you had enough money to afford it.

So I was lucky. Within a couple years of getting out of college I had landed a job in one of the fastest-growing industries on the planet. I was effectively a contributor to the expansion of the technology revolution during the beginning stages of what some consider unbelievable growth.

Although the introduction and growth of the new technologies we see today are awe-inspiring compared to the technologies introduced during the late 1980s and throughout the 1990s, it was a very strange time for most people in industrialized nations. It was the first time we were exposed to an abundance of information and the different types of technologies that could deliver it. I remember going to my father and asking if everything had gone so fast when he was my age. His response startled me. He looked at me and said, "Not like this." At that point in my life, I realized that we were living in a new age. We had gone from a time of limited access to information to overwhelming abundance and availability—and that was in 1993.

It was an amazing time. I could now access information by going to a computer and typing in a few keystrokes; I could learn anything I wanted to learn. While driving (without wires), I could keep in touch with friends, family, and everyone else who mattered. I was almost unconsciously being absorbed into a new world of connectivity that would change my life forever.

I know that getting information from a computer is just not that amazing anymore, but what's amazing is that it was only twenty years ago that the average individual did not have that type of access to information. The infusion of information technology has definitely impacted all of our lives in various ways and has ushered in a whole new set of opportunities and challenges.

I've considered the past twenty years as fertile ground for what appears to be unlimited forms of opportunity for those living in industrialized nations. I'm deeply grateful because I've received tremendous benefits from this new revolution. However, with those new opportunities, we have also been challenged with a new problem that the architects of the information age may not have considered: *too much information.*

A MAJOR CAUSE OF LOW PERFORMANCE

Let me start out by describing a really big problem, a problem that can also be viewed as one of the greatest phenomena of our time: the information superhighway!

Due to the growth of communications technologies and the availability of different tools like personal computers, PDAs and the Internet, we have been bombarded with multiple media that can be used to educate and by some to influence, mislead, and downright manipulate us. Living in an industrialized nation, this can be a constant bombardment of information and product marketing twenty-four hours a day, seven days a week. While this perpetual flow of information can open doors and create opportunity, it is also very easy for us to get distracted by its abundance. And often times we're getting distracted by individuals and organizations trying to market things that we really don't need or want.

Most of the information we encounter on the web is not necessarily developed to simply educate and inform. As a responsible consumer, if you don't *consciously* think about the information you are consuming, you are going to be influenced and may receive information that brings little value to your future success. An overabundance of miscellaneous information can really become a distraction. People who develop and distribute free content usually have a social, economic, or political agenda. Be even more careful if information is being provided or promoted with intent to get you to make a buying decision or to take action. Just go to any online search engine and do a search based on your interests; you will see that the vast majority of the websites are selling something.

Beware of the Television in Your Pocket!

When we watch TV for more than ten minutes, we will see advertisements. When we are driving our cars, we (sometime unconsciously) see billboards that attempt to influence our buying decisions. And now, the next medium that is destined to have an overwhelming impact on our buying decisions and daily thinking processes is the mobile phone. It's already started. There are organizations and industries participating in a shared think tank, developing ways to use our mobile phones to influence our buying decisions, habits, and ways of thinking. Just wait! Soon your phone will be your wallet too.[1] The bottom line is, we are always being influenced—even if it's a passive influence.

Filtering Information Can Save Your Future

I'm saying that this is one of the biggest problems of our time; never in history have we been exposed to so many different types of information coming to us so fast using so many different, powerfully influential, media. It gets to us in all forms: everything from video, audio, and traditional written content. Actually, the marketing community targets as many of our senses as they can in order to communicate their message. If you don't pull back and decide to know what *you* really want to know, you are destined for failure.

If you want good, quality information that will make a difference in your life, educate you, and take you to the next level, you need to know how to filter out unnecessary information and focus on consuming *premium quality* information that is related to what you want out of life. Your success in the future will be based on how well you can filter information as well as target and leverage that information to create an action plan for success based on your goals

---

1 Please note that I've been an active participant in both the marketing and telecommunications industries for the last twenty years. I'm excited about the growth of mobile phones and PDAs; immediate access to information is a gift for our generation. The technologies that deliver information are not the problem; not taking individual responsibility to control the inflow of information is.

and aspirations. In other words, the key to getting focused on what matters most is learning how to harness the information technology tools you use every day to filter out useless information and attract information that can have an astoundingly positive impact on your future.

THREE ESSENTIAL STEPS

You may never know what results come of your action,
but if you do nothing there will be no result.
—Mahatma Gandhi

Being successful in just about any endeavor takes three essential steps. Simple but not easy, these steps are critical to high performance. Most people never complete the first step because it's the most time-consuming and will challenge your way of thinking the most. Nonetheless, not doing it will drastically reduce your chances of getting High Octane Performance (HOP) results. Many studies have proven that a mere 3 percent of the population sets goals and roughly 1 percent actually writes them down. The first step using the HOP method will help you start writing (or sketching).

Using an animated and unique analogy, I will walk you through the three steps to developing a lifestyle of High Octane Performance.

- **Step 1: Get Focused**
  You will learn how to eliminate distractions and target the few things that make a difference to your success. Getting focused on what matters most will help you set ambitious, realistic, and obtainable goals in the most important areas of your life.

- **Step 2: Determine Your Destination**
  Develop a road map for success. Learn the secret to eliminating the roadblocks that can prevent you from high performance. Gain access to the information you need to win any race within thirty to ninety days.

- **Step 3: Take Action and Measure Performance**
  Take the challenge that will change your life forever! Take action! Work with the determination that you will win the race.

DEFINING YOUR MISSION

Life's Greatest Endeavor

A society in which vocation and job are separated for most people gradually creates an economy that is often devoid of spirit, one that frequently fills our pocketbooks at the cost of emptying our souls.
—*Sam Keen*

Answer this question before you move on:

If money was not an issue, and you were in a race to win, what type of car would you drive?

Answer that question before you keep reading!

IMPORTANT

You will cheat yourself if you don't stop and really do this.

When you were thinking about it, was your choice based on performance, economy, or comfort? I'm sure the ideal situation would be a combination of the three. But to win the race, did you choose a really cheap, economical car, or did you choose a top-quality, high-performance car like a Maserati or BMW (cars known to deliver speed and performance)? The point is that if you are in the race to win, you should choose a vehicle that's built to win the race. We all know that the fastest cars are expected to have engines that can perform under extreme conditions.

This book was designed for people with High Octane Performance engines; people who believe they were born to make a difference on this planet before they die. Regardless of your circumstances, background, or starting point, deciding to have the right engine for the journey will help you win the race of life. After you have decided that you have a High Octane Performance engine, the road becomes clear, your life's engine goes into high gear, your internal navigation system kicks in, those perfectly engineered tires grip the road, and you are off to win any race.

OK, please forgive me, I'm getting a little ahead of myself! Before we get started, let me tell you more about the target audience for this book.

Was This Book Meant for You?

This information is intended for a very small group of people. I am writing to those whom W.E.B Du Bois referred to as the "talented tenth," a small group of individuals who are responsible for making positive contributions to society.[2] These are individuals dedicated to improving the lives and livelihood of those less fortunate or less capable.

---

2 See http://en.wikipedia.org/wiki/The_Talented_Tenth. Although Du Bois used this phrase to specifically identify a small group of leaders within a specific ethnic group, I believe that there is a talented 10 percent of society that's responsible for stepping up and leading regardless of race, religion, or nationality.

The objective of this book is to help those in that talented 10 percent (which hopefully includes you) get the results they were meant to achieve in life. This is all presented in an animated way of looking at your life so you can set realistic goals and take action.

So let's determine if this book was written for you. Keep in mind that if you answer *no* to the first question below, then you may be wasting your time reading this book.[3]

- *Do you have a High Octane Performance engine?*
- *When you look at yourself, do you consider yourself to be a high performer in life?*
- *How do you measure success?*
- *Do you know what you are supposed to do with your life?*
- *Do your friends and family know what you are supposed to do with your life?*
- *Do you know how to effectively develop a team of individuals dedicated to helping you get to your life's destination?*
- *Do you have specific short-term and long-term goals?*
- *Do you have a clear plan or road map for your goals?*
- *Do you believe that you were meant to do great things?*

Keep in mind that while I'm asking these questions, I'm not expecting you to have all the answers right now. If you do, great! But if you don't, it doesn't matter because I intend to share a unique animated model that you can use to effectively answer the above questions within thirty days and have a plan for a life full of high-performance accomplishments well into your retirement, creating a legacy that will live on when you are no longer part of the human race. However, the plan will not work unless you have consciously decided that you have a High Octane Performance engine. Committing to

---

3 It's simply a decision. This book can only help you if you are committed to high performance.

High Octane Performance is a decision that you are deciding to stick with until you die. Making that decision alone will change your life forever.

My Disclaimer

Please note that I am not asking you if you consider yourself to be successful or not. I want to know if you believe that you are meant to perform at the highest levels of your ability. Let me be clear: at this point, I'm not even trying to encourage you. This is absolutely not meant to be some personal development rant or meant to motivate you to desire more out of life. There's plenty of positive mental attitude stuff out there and this book is not meant to serve that market. I'm not even trying to tell you that you *should* have a high-performance engine or that you *should* be the best that you can be. That is absolutely not the goal here. I'm saying that this book is not meant for you if you don't already have that burning desire to do something, be somebody, or make a difference in the lives of others before you die.

This book will help you gain clarity on what you are meant to do in your life. Using an animated approach to goal setting, you will be able to focus on the essential activities that will help you develop your compass.[4] After gaining a clear understanding of your general direction in life, you will be able to create a thirty-day action plan that will empower you to make progress toward your life's purpose, measure your performance, make changes, and reset your compass when necessary.

---

4 See http://en.wikipedia.org/wiki/Compass. Like a real compass, it's important that you already have or develop a sense of direction for your purpose in life.

Stop Again!

Before we move forward and get into first gear, it is important that you make that decision now.

So—do you have a High Octane Performance engine?

If you are one of those folks who says they are satisfied with where they are in life right now, then you really don't need to read the rest of this book. It will be a waste of your time. Hand it to somebody who needs to go to the next level; someone who needs to reset his self-confidence and belief system. Give it to someone who knows that she is meant for greatness but doesn't know where to start.

On the other hand, if you have a high-performance engine and already have a clear idea of what you want to do with your life, you may want to consider reading on. If you already have the mental clarity and have already reaped the benefits of a High Octane Performance engine, then this book will help you development a format to help others get to where you are. The rest of this book will give you a way of relating to and understanding other people; a way to visually see their goals and dreams so that you can support them, collaborate with them, and inspire them to high performance.

Are you capable of performing at high levels?

The answer to that question depends on what you have decided about your future. I argue that everyone born into this world is capable of having a high-performance engine. Some may argue that physical, mental, social, economical, or political circumstances can play a large role in the opportunities available to everyone individually. So it's really not fair to say that *everyone* is capable of having a High Octane Performance engine.

I simply believe that measuring performance in your life is based on your own definition of performance. It should not be compared to someone else's definition. Success can be measured based on hitting goals that *you* have decided in advance, and performance is based on how long it took *you* to get there when you hit the goal.

This is important!

You are responsible for creating your own definition of success. Simply put, not everyone's engine is created the same. Some folks are capable of producing a whole lot more in certain areas than others because of the talents and abilities they we were given at birth. Every individual on this planet has his own customized engine, capable of performing at the highest levels of his God-given talents. Knowing, understanding, and believing in those talents makes all the difference in the world. Unfortunately, the vast majority of people don't know how to fine-tune their talents in order to achieve the highest levels of performance. In most cases, success and High Octane Performance is simply a secret that the vast majority of people will never know. I plan to let you in on that secret in this book.

If the success that you have been seeking eludes you, consider the following hypotheses. What you have been told about yourself, your beliefs and the things that shape your worldview, may be the very reason you are being held back from incredible success. As I alluded to earlier, the folks marketing to you, educating you, singing to you, entertaining you, and preaching to you may be influencing your failure; that's why learning how to filter information is a big part of your key to success and High Octane Performance in the future.

Before I move into second gear and start giving you the secret, I need a commitment from you. Simply believe that success in your lifetime (based on your own definition of it) is possible. What separates people who succeed and people who don't succeed is simply how they view themselves, the world, and what they believe is possible.

It's Possible!

GETTING FOCUSED

Make Sure Your Engine Is Prepared To Win!

The first step is to learn how to get focused. Remember, you chose a vehicle that's built to win. Cars that win races don't win because they simply look sleek, cool, or have the best design. They win because they have engines engineered to perform at high levels under extreme conditions. The secret to getting top results from high-performing engines is using fuel with the right octane.[5] Later in this book I will address what fuel represents based on this analogy. For now, let's agree that your engine requires the highest-quality fuel available, and that's what you are committed to using.

Completing this first step is essential to winning any race in life. There is a reason that most of society never gets this done: it's hard to do because it takes time and discipline. Again, this book was designed for the minority that will make the time and have the internal desire to get it done.

---

5 This is a really important point. Do a Google search for "high octane engines" or go to http://auto.howstuffworks.com/fuel-efficiency/fuel-consumption/question90.htm to better understand the relationship between high-performing engines and the fuel needed to power them. Remember, this is simply an analogy. Don't get caught up with the technical aspects of how it works. The big picture is that high octane fuel powers engines that were designed for high performance.

THE CAR

Design Your Life

Most personal development, motivational, or inspirational materials cover the following essential areas:

- Developing a mission or purpose
- Setting goals
- Creating and implementing an action plan

While it would be great if you receive motivational and inspirational benefits from reading this book, it was not written for that purpose. Again, the purpose of this book is to get you focused on what matters most to you and to help you clarify your purpose, then help you put together a high-performance road map that will help you get to that destination. I guess some folks would call that *personal development*, but I believe that the starting point for all forms of personal development is clarifying where you are and determining a destination—in other words, knowing your mission. After you know who you are and where you are going, the personal effort it takes to get to your destination is what I consider personal development. Any efforts toward self-improvement without first clarifying and understanding your mission will likely lead to failure.

Using simple tools, this book will guide you through clarifying your mission and help you design realistic, achievable goals using the High Octane Performance (HOP) method.

Since this method is based on a car analogy, let's review some of the major components of a "typical" car.

The above icons—components of a car—will be used to represent specific areas in your life that are essential when designing a life plan. Have fun and add any other components that you believe are essential, but for the purposes of this plan, we will focus on the five listed above. This book is organized in a way to help you get focused first by brainstorming on specific areas in your life that impact you on a daily basis. The essential first step is identifying and clarifying what is important to you, which will also help you more clearly define your mission; we will refer to this as your *engine*. It's a good chance that the things you currently do every day, unconsciously, can provide an insight to your life's purpose and help you develop a road map for High Octane Performance.

THE ENGINE

How Do You Know What You're Supposed to Do with Your Life?

The engine of a car can be compared to your mission or purpose in life. An engine is really a highly engineered work of art. It's responsible for mixing gasoline, air, and oil to deliver the needed performance to keep a car powered after ignition. While this book is intended to help you clarify your mission, it will not *give* you a mission or purpose. I believe everyone's mission in life is God-given; your relationship with God will ultimately help you know what you are supposed to do with your life.

Doing the following exercise will serve as a practical guide to helping you more clearly understand what's important to you. It's not about me suggesting or telling you the purpose of your life; it's about you going through an exercise to get clarity on what is happening in your life right now and identifying the things that bombard your thinking processes every day.

So let's start by challenging you to do an exercise that can take some considerable time.

CAUTION

This exercise could change the way you think about what's going on in our life.

Make Sure You Do It Now!

As you go through this exercise, please keep in mind that it's the beginning of the process. It's necessary that you spend quality time reviewing the essential areas of your life that could impact your future. This could take some time. You are about to sit down for a predetermined period of time and think about your current and future financial situation; consider what you already know (about life) and determine what you want to learn; resolve who is really important to you and the type of relationships you want to maintain in the future; and make decisions about your future health and physical lifestyle. Again, this is only the beginning of the process. Don't expect to perform at high levels immediately after you are done with this first exercise.

THE WHEELS

The Four Areas of Your Life You Can't Ignore.

There are four areas in our lives that we make decisions about every day. Some of us do it consciously; most of us do it unconsciously. Every day, we're making decisions in the areas of finance, education, personal relationships and health. For example, if you don't consciously think about your current monetary situation and make plans for at least basic economic survival, you are making a decision that will impact your future financial well-being. By ignoring it or simply not thinking about it, you're making a decision to ignore your financial stability. Over time, that ignorance or unconscious decision making can lead to poverty and other unfortunate conditions. Ultimately, the decisions you make in one area of your life will influence the decisions you make in the other three areas.

The four wheels represent four key aspects of your life:

- Your Financial Wheel
- Your Educational Wheel
- Your Relationship Wheel
- Your Health Wheel

When it comes to the inflow of information, if you don't consciously organize your thoughts regarding the things that you want to know or learn, you will be bombarded with information coming from all aspects of your life. Remember, there are people out there who are constantly focused on marketing and influencing our thoughts. So if you don't consciously organize your thoughts, they're likely to be organized by someone else.

The whole point of using the analogy of a car is that the four wheels represent those four aspects of our lives that we consciously or unconsciously make decisions about every day. A flat tire in either of these areas will cause problems with the other tires and eventually the whole vehicle—that is, your entire life. Just as you can't drive a car very far with a flat tire, you may have issues trying to live a "normal" life if you have major issues in any one of these areas. So if you have been making unconscious decisions regarding your financial life, educational growth, personal relationships or health, stop it now. Take the time to dissect these areas of your life and commit to making conscious, solid decisions in those areas. By doing this alone, you will gain a sense of control in your life and begin the process of filtering information.

Here's the Challenge

Sit down for four hours, or at least for four one-hour sessions, and map out in your mind each of these four areas of your life. Look at each wheel and come up with as many possibilities as you can brainstorm. Use the companion worksheets listed as the beginning of this book to help you generate ideas, jar your memory, and make the exercise a manageable task. I recommend that you stop after reading each of the following sections and do the suggested exercise for that section. After you get started, you may find that each area of your life is full of complexity. Make sure you dedicate at least an hour for each section. The longer you spend brainstorming for each area of your life, the more likely you will exhaust the possibilities and gather enough information so that you can be successful at identifying specific things that are essential for each wheel.

Get a clean sheet of paper and start mind mapping the spokes of each wheel. If you have trouble doing this by yourself, now is a good time to find a life coach or someone who can help you complete the exercise.[6] At this point, getting help from someone else is not absolutely necessary; however, later in this book you will have an exercise that will require honest feedback from a confidant or life coach. So it's a good idea to start looking for someone to work with now.

Here's a good example of how your wheels should look. Keep it simple, but make sure you come up with at least three spokes or areas for potential growth.

I've found that good old-fashioned pencil and paper does the job, but if you are a "techie" and would like some software applications, do a web search for "mind-mapping software" and you will find several options, some of them free. I recommend the iMindMap6 software, which was developed by the originator of the concept of mind mapping, Tony Buzan.

---

6 Working on this exercise with a life coach will be helpful. However, make sure you give a copy of this book to your coach so you both agree to follow the plan and the methods described here.

Tony is the world's foremost expert on thinking visually, and a leading lecturer on the brain and learning. Tony has lectured to diverse audiences, ranging from large corporations to universities to governments. Tony invented mind mapping in the 1970s, and has been instructing millions in this technique ever since. The mind map is a visual representation of the thought process, and became instantly popular as a creative, innovative and efficient alternative to linear notation. The mind map is an adaptable tool for just about anything: planning, organizing, creating, presenting, problem solving, communicating and much more!

Warning: Using software for this exercise can sometimes complicate the process and get in the way of progress. If it takes you more than twenty minutes to setup and get started using software, back away and use pencil and paper.

Get It Done!

YOUR FINANCIAL WHEEL

If you would be wealthy, think of saving as well as getting.
—Benjamin Franklin

The fundamental aspects of your financial wheel are that you have an income, you spend money to live, and you reserve some money for the future. Regardless of how much money you have right now, these fundamentals are among the basic essentials of daily living.

Income Source

You may have a job, provide a service, sell a product, or run a successful business; or you may have invented something. A consistent income is imperative. At this point, it does not matter how much you make; it just matters that you are generating some sort of income.

Consider this: you're moving through life, and you're creating a situation in your life that will affect you and everybody who depends on you. I call this your *financial wheel*. I'm suggesting that you take the time, dissect that wheel. Detail all of the ways that you make money, all of the ways that you spend money, all of the things you do to create wealth, and all of the potential income ideas and possibilities. Below are at least three areas that you should consider including in your diagram.

Expenses You may have heard the saying, "The only things certain in life are death a nd taxes." Well, expenses should be added to that, because these days, we all have expenses. Check out the companion worksheet to get an idea of common expenses and make sure you include those that pertain to your situation.

Wealth Creation

This includes things like your car, your house, and anything you have that holds value. Wikipedia defines wealth as the abundance of valuable resources or material possessions. The bottom line is, if you have an income and you subtract expenses, whatever is left over can be considered a form of wealth.

Future Ideas for Creating Income

This is important because it can lead to massive success or dismal failure. If you are a dreamer, inventor, or entrepreneur, you must include this as part of your financial wheel. You may have multiple ideas, inventions, and businesses. It is a good chance that the more creative you are, the more likely you are to have a difficult time focusing on one idea and making it successful before moving on to the next idea. Multiple ideas, business ventures, or opportunities can be the biggest form of distraction and lead to low performance overall. Make sure you really brainstorm here and include as many ideas and potential business ventures as possible.

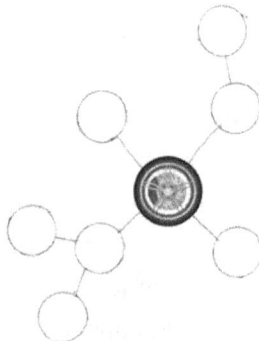

Warning: Don't skip this part just because you already have a financial or accounting adviser. In fact, if you use professionals, I recommend that you call them, set an appointment, and have them complete this exercise with you. Just keep in mind that you are not looking for them to provide you with a nice-looking report with graphs and diagrams. The goal here is for you to create a simple diagram that looks similar to a wheel with spokes. This diagram that you create will be important when you meet with your life coach or confidant later. Completing this exercise alone can have an overwhelmingly positive impact on your future. This will help you create a plan that will help you achieve your goals as well as make you aware of your financial standing so you can make conscious financial decisions from now on.

Do This Now!

YOUR EDUCATIONAL WHEEL

The more you know, the more you know you don't know.
—Aristotle

Your *educational wheel* represents all the knowledge you've acquired since birth. The second you were conceived (or at least started developing a brain) you began learning different things from a variety of sources. Research suggests that we even learn at those early stages of life; we begin hearing and feeling things and getting information from our parents that we may not consciously realize at the time.

After you were born, you started learning and gathering information on your own, using your five senses. In other words, you know what you know because of the information you have been exposed to since childhood. This represents your body of knowledge.

Your educational wheel is a representation of what you know. Philosophers have tackled and debated this topic of how we know what we know for hundreds of years; it's called *epistemology*. While this could be an engaging subject to study and help you learn more about yourself, I'm not suggesting that you spend lots of time pondering everything you know. It's not *what you know already* that matters; performing at high levels is all about identifying *what you want to know.*

For this exercise, focus on what you want to know. Mind map or draw out the spokes of your educational wheel by detailing what you would like to learn. It could be anything. Spend time identifying all of the things you've ever wanted to know. Don't be intimidated by this activity; ignore the urge to leave out something because you think it's complicated or above your capacity to learn. The simple goal here is to map out all of the things that you would be interested in learning if you had the time and ability. The more exhaustive the list, the more likely you are to be successful at identifying the essential things you will need to learn in order to get on the road to High Octane Performance in all of the areas of your life.

By spending at least an hour on this exercise you will start the process of taking responsibility of your *conscious* information flow and it will help you develop a filter to block information that's not really necessary for your future growth and High Performance.

When you take full responsibility for your educational wheel, you will be more aware of information and how it impacts all of your senses. Remember I suggested earlier in this book that there are other individuals, groups, and organizations out there that want to influence your thinking and buying decisions. Being actively aware of your senses and what you are learning will reduce the effectiveness of these entities and their influence on your everyday life. It will allow you to sift out information and marketing efforts that are not in your future best interest. The bottom line is, this exercise will help you develop your ability to filter out bad information and focus on consuming the information that will make a positive difference in your life.

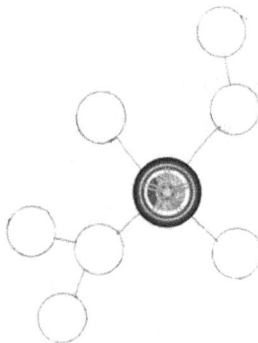

Do This Now!

YOUR RELATIONSHIP WHEEL

Stanley Milgram originally coined the term "six degrees of separation" in 1967 to show that everyone in the modern world was capable of connecting to another by linking people and interests.

When thinking about relationships, think about the people in your life who are so important to you that you are motivated to consciously invest in them and improve your relationship with them every single day.

Saying the simple phrase "I love you" to someone in that small inner circle of folks that make up your relationship wheel could be the biggest return on investment in terms of building strong relationships. You are really investing in that person and creating a reciprocal environment. The phrase "I love you" is so simple that we probably don't use it enough and take it for granted. For example, if you are fortunate enough to see someone you love every day, it's easy to take that relationship for granted.

Try This!

Go to someone you love deeply; touch him or her on the shoulder and say, "You know what? I love you and just wanted to let you know you're important to me because of…"

Be careful! The response you get can tell you lots about your relationship with that person.

Regardless of the response, making a conscious and consistent effort to simply say "I love you" will change your life forever and add to the performance of your relationship wheel.

In the early 1990s, when I first started adopting the analogy between car parts and the essential areas in our lives that impact us every day, the Internet was not yet available to the general public. So the idea of recommending that someone create an exhaustive list of everyone they knew was a daunting task, especially if one were to consider the idea of six degrees of separation; it could be a pretty long list. However, it's much easier these days because of social networking applications like LinkedIn, Facebook, and Google Plus (among others). These applications have allowed us to do a better job at keeping in touch with people around us and they keeps us connected with an extended network of hundreds or even thousands of people. These are also relationships that should be considered when you are mapping out the spokes of your relationship wheel.

So let's get to what you will need to do for this exercise. How do you put together a good relationship wheel?

Answer the following questions:

- Who would you die for? (I know, it's a pretty big question.)
- Who do you want to spend the rest of your life knowing?
- Do you have a confidant or someone you can tell everything and anything to?
- Do you have someone you consider your soul mate?
- Do you have friends or relatives who depend on you for their well-being?
- Do have a mentor?
- Do you have a mastermind group, team, organization or association of people whom you go to for feedback and advice? (I call this your *steering committee*.)

Over the past twenty years, as a High Octane Performance coach, I've had people cry in front of me because they couldn't think of anyone to put on this wheel. We all have different circumstances, and our network of friends, family, and associations is unique from person to person. If you get stuck here, this is a good time to reach out to a life coach for help. You need to find at least one person who you can work with in order to complete this exercise.

Don't skip this exercise—it's critical to your success.

So if you sit down and think about it long enough (set aside at least an hour), you will start thinking of the people most important to you and build the spokes of your relationship wheel. It's been my experience that most people will include their spouse, a significant other, or a parent. Just about everybody with children will include a child or all of their children. In some cases people will include siblings. The goal is to fill your wheel with people you really care about. However, if coming up with people you love is a difficult task, you need to at least find three people with whom you would like to learn how to love and build a relationship with.

Do This Now!

YOUR HEALTH AND FITNESS WHEEL

"When health is absent, wisdom cannot reveal itself, art cannot become manifest, strength cannot be exerted, wealth is useless, and reason is powerless."
- Herophiles

I won't pretend to be a guru so I'm including the definitions of health and fitness as defined by Wikipedia—the source for all information, all the time. We all know that if it came from the Internet, it must be true. Hmmm…maybe not.

Health is the level of functional or metabolic efficiency of a living being. In humans, it is the general condition of a person's mind and body, usually meaning to be free from illness, injury or pain (as in "good health" or "healthy").

Physical fitness comprises two related concepts: general fitness (a state of health and well-being), and specific fitness (a task-oriented definition based on the ability to perform specific aspects of sports or occupations). Physical fitness is generally achieved through correct nutrition, exercise, and rest.

Considering all of the information on weight loss, performance enhancement programs, personal training gurus and fitness industries, I'll try to keep it simple. Regardless of which program you choose to purchase or whomever you decided to work with to obtain your goals, one of the most important things you can do is commit to maintaining good health and developing a sustainable fitness plan—for life.

Usually, at the beginning of the year, we include getting slim, working out, or going to the gym in our list of New Year's resolutions. So at the start of the year, we are excited about our new goals and we are motivated to make changes and do some exercise. However, for most of us, sustaining that effort or keeping that resolution becomes challenging as we get to the second and third months of the year. Consider these statistics from Quara.com on the number of people who give up on their New Year's resolutions shortly after the start of the year:

12% of new gym members join in January, presumably in an effort to make good on New Year's resolutions. Some clubs see an increase of 30–50% in January.

Health clubs in the U.S. had more than 50 million members and revenue of $20.3 billion in 2010.... But clubs reported that members typically visit only 54 times or slightly less than once a week.

50% of all new health club members quit within the first six months of signing up according to the International Health, Racquet & Sports Club Association. By March new member attendance has diminished "considerably."

A study by the American Economic Review that surveyed nearly 8,000 members over a three year period found gym-goers who paid per visit, rather than paying monthly, saved an average of $600.

Setting a simple goal to go to the gym or exercise more often is not good enough if you want to "consistently" maintain good health. Being healthy and fit means permanently changing your lifestyle so you don't have to make false commitments at the beginning of every year.

Don't miss this point. If you want to improve your health, make a commitment to do the following two things:

1. At least walk or do some type of exercise every day (if you can).
2. Learn what happens to your body when you consume different types of foods and commit to *consciously* managing your diet for the rest of your life. Hint: think twice before your eat something that doctors say children, pregnant women, or people with diabetes should not eat.

There's a lot of controversy about the different foods we should and should not eat. This book was not written to advocate or promote any specific view. It's just critical that you are aware of the fact that the food you eat will affect you every single day. Not consciously developing a diet plan for long-term health maintenance combined with poor exercise habits can absolutely impact your performance.

The whole idea of the health wheel is to get you to set goals in this area and motivate you to develop the right eating and exercise habits so that you can experience a more well-rounded physical life. If your health wheel has problems, it will certainly impact the other wheels of your car.

Finding a good fitness coach or personal trainer and someone who understands the affects of food intake (like a nutritionist or even your doctor) will be critical to your success and will help you make strides toward completing this exercise. However, if you are like me, Google is a good option as well, but you will have to sift through bogus and inaccurate content to find reliable "premium" information that will give you the results you are seeking. Just keep in mind that the right experts or professionals can help you navigate through bogus information and save lots of time.

So here's how you approach this exercise. Brainstorm to create a list of things you would like to accomplish physically. Don't forget to do this using a wheel and spoke diagram similar to your activities for your other wheels—the other areas of your life. Since we all have unique capability and inability, make sure you list things that you can reasonably accomplish but make sure you also include some things that could make you stretch a little. For example, if you are healthy and your body can handle the stress, consider completing a mini-triathlon, marathon, or sports event as a goal. Or it could be taking a particular sport or activity and deciding to master the fundamentals. Again, you are not competing with anyone else. You want to set obtainable goals that you can be accomplish within a thirty - to ninety -day time period. Spend quality time and exhaust the possibilities of things you can accomplish. You can even create spokes for things that you would like to do at some point in your life but can't imagine yourself doing right now.

Understanding Food

Make sure you study how the following types of foods affect your body and clearly understand why they are essential for maintaining good health:

- Carbohydrates
- Proteins
- Fats
- Water
- Sugar
- Salt

Although I recommend that you spend a considerable amount of time (ideally, the rest of your life) researching and learning the affects of the above listed foods, for the purpose of this exercise, I simply recommend that you become somewhat familiar with each of them. Many of the common causes of disease in our bodies stem from a lack or overabundance of these foods or products that contain them.

Spend thirty minutes and do this exercise now; then spend another thirty minutes studying food.

There are lots of different beliefs and theories on how to be healthy and which fitness plans you should implement. The goal of the exercise is to create a plan or find one that you would like to implement. Synthesizing information from different sources is a good idea. Just keep in mind that no one has the secret sauce to perfect health. What works for someone else may not work for you.

Do This Now!

Consider reaching out for professional help with this exercise.

YOUR STEERING WHEEL

Getting Help

Your steering wheel represents the people around you who will help you hit your goals and stay on track. There are different ways to develop a team of people who are willing to help you perform at high levels, support your mission, and hold you accountable to fulfilling your life's purpose.

The following are a list of ways to strategically create a community of friends, family, and associates who can help you stay focused.

- Reach out to the top three individuals you listed on your relationship wheel
- Start a mastermind group – recruit individuals with specialized expertise in your areas of need
- Hire a life coach
- Find a HOP Coach (someone who's familiar with the HOP method) or give your life coach this book.

Keep this in mind: when you are requesting support from others, you are responsible for being able to effectively communicate what matters most to you so your virtual "steering committee" can support you. Hopefully, this book will help you develop an easy format for communicating your dreams, goals, and aspirations. It's been my experience that the car analogy will help others visually see your life in a relatable way. So doing the exercises in this book should help you more effectively design a road map that can be easily expressed to your support team.

When you are telling someone else your story and recruiting your team, make sure you cover the following:

Your Car	**Areas of your life**
Engine	Share your mission or life's purpose. This can be a single statement or a whole paragraph.
Financial Wheel	Everything related to income, expenses, and accumulation of wealth. This should be shared with someone you trust who can help you improve your current situation.
Education Wheel	Share the top five things you want to learn that are related to your mission or life's purpose.
Relationship Wheel	Identify the top three people in your life. You can list more, but make sure you identify the people you are committed to sharing your life with for the rest of your life.
Health Wheel	Describe least three goals you have that will improve your overall health and require a reasonable amount of fitness-related activity.

SET SPECIFIC & MEASURABLE GOALS

- Look at each area in your life and choose one thing that you want to improve or change within 30 days. Write it down and make sure it's something that you can really accomplish within a thirty day timeframe. It has to be measurable and specific.
- Determine what you need to learn or do in order to make this goal achievable.
- Get feedback from your confidants, coaches, mentors and advisors
- Broadcast it - commit to it by telling somebody about it. Let your support system know that you have a goal that you want to achieve within 30 days.

TAKING ACTION & MEASURE PERFORMANCE

Take the challenge that will change your life forever! Take action! Act with the determination that you will win the race.

I have developed a website called the Thirty-Day Success Challenge at http://www.30daysuccesschallenge.com. It's now time for you to take action. You are invited to take the challenge and announce your new destination to the world. While this adds a little pressure, it reinforces your motivation to move forward and get results. After all, when you tell the world you are going to do something, your integrity is on the line.

Do You Do What You Say You Are Going to Do?

After you post your Thirty-Day Success Challenge, you will get access to a community of other people who are undertaking their own challenges. It's simple—tell us your challenge and we will help you build a community around getting it done. We will also invite you to help build a support community for others using the HOP method.

DON'T FORGET TO CHANGE YOUR OIL!

In any car, whether a well-engineered one or not, changing the oil is essential to longevity and continued high performance. Use the following schedule to set and review your goals. It's like changing the oil in your car: if you don't do it, your engine will have problems down the road. What follows is one of the most common questions when setting goals.

How Do I Determine What Goal to Set?

If you have taken the time to mind map your wheels, it's as simple as selecting one of the spokes of each wheel and deciding to set a deadline to get it done. For example, if you are setting a thirty-day goal, make sure you find something within each major area of your life (each wheel) and determine what it takes to get it done within that thirty-day period.

The Maintenance Schedule

The following is a recommended schedule for sitting down to reset your goals, or what I call *changing the oil*.

- **Immediately:** After reading this book, take a look back at your goals.
- **After thirty days:** "Kick your tires" and see how you are doing.

- **Every ninety days:** Change the oil; and sit down with your HOP coach.
- **Every year:** Due minor maintenance; review everything and make sure you are on track to hit some of your life's goals within a three- to five-year time frame. This is an intrusive process, and I highly recommend either a HOP coach or a life coach who understands the HOP method.
- **Every three years:** Overhaul; look at everything in your life and make sure your goals, dreams, and aspirations are in line with your mission or purpose. This requires deep soul searching and introspection. After you do this the first time the right way, it becomes easier to do every three years. Not much will change. You are simply making sure your compass is working. Keep in mind that astronauts are off track 99% of the time when they are going to the moon. It is the constant recalculations and realignment with the goal of landing on the moon that get them there and back successfully.

THE SECRET FORMULA: FUEL

Burning 93 octane fuel—ultimately, what you believe about yourself and your purpose in life—has lots to do with how successful you are or will be in the future. Ultimately, your spiritual relationship will make all the difference in the world. Since this is not a book on religion, I'm not advocating that you join any specific religious institution or subscribe to any specific theology or philosophy that describes God or a supreme being. I'm simply suggesting that you become deeply interested in what you already believe and why you believe it. Pondering who you are, what you believe, and why you believe are worthy lifelong causes. I believe sincere interest in the study of epistemology will help you gain clarity on why you believe what you believe and will help you get closer to understanding your purpose or mission in life.

After reading many religious and spiritual books (even then, probably not enough of them), I've come to the conclusion that anyone sincerely searching for the answers to who God is or answers to the universe and the source of our existence will probably end up with more questions than answers. So, I will not use this book as a platform to advocate or promote any theological or philosophical view. However, to remain consistent with the analogy of a car, I will spend a little bit of time explaining how the fuel that you put into your car has a lot to do with performance.

Earlier in this book, when you chose to have a high-performance car with a high-performance engine, you also (consciously or unconsciously) made a choice to use the highest "octane" fuel. While octane ratings for most cars come in grades of 87, 89, and 93, most high-performing race cars require an even higher octane. The higher octane increases the race car's efficiency and prevents damage by controlling how gasoline combusts in the engine.

While studying octane and the history of octane levels can be an interesting and engaging subject for some, for the purposes of this analogy, I will focus on the octane levels that gas stations in the United States make available to the general public: 87, 89, and 93.

Compared to the other areas of your life, your spiritual life is unique in that it can't be measured by anyone other than you. Each of the other areas of your life can be measured and counted. For example, you either have an abundance of money or you don't. You have either obtained a finite quantity of information or you have not. You either have a certain number of friends, family members, and associates or you do not. You either have good health (without disease) and you are fit or you are not. All of those things are quantifiable in some way or another. Your spiritual life arguably has no quantification. No one else can look at you and determine how spiritual you are; it's simply something each of us as individuals has to determine on our own. That's the beauty of spirituality. How much of it you have depends solely on you.

Considering the above statements, I will use our car analogy to describe different levels of spirituality in order to explain what I mean by the *octane* in High Octane Performance. This is likely to be the most controversial part of this book, so please be patient.

Burning 87 Octane Fuel

Everybody has to burn at least 87 octane fuel to join the race of life. It's my opinion that everyone has some form of spirituality; even if you don't believe in God or the existence of a supreme being, you still have a spiritual life. Whatever you believe provides enough substance to argue that you are a spiritual creature of some sort. Using the car analogy, 87 octane is the lowest grade of gas available; some would argue that it is the dirtiest grade of gas. Regardless, if you put gas in a properly functioning car, the car will move. How fast and for how long it will move depends on how long it takes for "dirty gas" to erode and have a negative impact on a vehicle that was intended for High Octane Performance.

Burning 89 Octane Fuel

Remember, this is simply an analogy, and if you research octane levels, you will find that there are various views on octane; choosing the grade you should use in your car depends on what's recommended by the manufacturer of that car. However, if you give me a little latitude to suggest that 87 octane represents your basic spiritual life, I would argue that 89 octane represents your religious life. It's a cleaner and higher grade of gas and should produce a higher level of performance.

Theology and various forms of religious-oriented ideology play a major role in the daily lives of people that live in most industrialized nations. It cannot be discounted that religious institutions and organizations play a major role in providing a foundation and environment for strong spiritual growth. However, they're just that: institutions designed to promote, support, and harvest the theology, ideology, and beliefs of particular religions. They are not a representation of your spiritual life. The reason I liken this to 89 octane is because like 89 octane, religion can provide a higher level of purity and quality to spirituality. But to be clear, religion and spirituality are not synonymous; they do not mean the same thing. I would argue that religion is a subset of spirituality. I understand that this point is debatable and some might argue the opposite. Again, this is simply an analogy. An octane level of 89 represents your willingness to adhere and commit to any institutionalized beliefs, including informal institutionalized beliefs. For example, a new wave of thinking by what some call the *New Thought* movement which promotes the belief that "like attracts like" and that by focusing on positive or negative thoughts one can bring about positive or negative results. People associated with the movement promote that there is a secret law of attraction that will bring into your life the positive or negative things that harbor within our thoughts. In other words, your thoughts have created your existing circumstances and influence your future. While there's some fascinating and positive aspects to this ideology, over time even this relatively new way of thinking will be regarded as a form of religion.

Burning 93 Octane Fuel

So let's discuss what it means to consistently burn 93 octane fuel. Burning 93 octane is simply making a *conscious* daily commitment to gaining clarity on your purpose or mission in life by having an unyielding desire to understand why you believe the things you believe.

What makes this a tough subject is that many of our beliefs are deeply rooted in religious ideology. There's nothing wrong with that. Regardless of your religions affiliation, I'm suggesting that you become committed to why you believe what you believe. It is my experience that if you set aside time to sincerely ponder why you believe what you believe about your relationship with God, you will gain clarity on the contributions you are responsible for making in society. I do think that what you believe will rule your entire life. The things you tell yourself everyday will influence your actions—and ultimately your results.

So what does it really mean to burn 93 octane? It is, quite simply, a relentless commitment to harness, control, and develop your spiritual growth. Proactively seek information and experiences that will enhance your spiritual awareness. Don't be passive. If you unconsciously allow extraneous information to seep into your daily thoughts, it will end up taking you in a direction that can easily challenge your purpose—and, in the end, your success in life.

Information Control: It's a Responsibility!

Knowing your purpose or mission in life helps you develop the filters needed for high performance. If you unconsciously allow extraneous information and marketing content to seep into your daily thoughts, you will end up making decisions that are not necessarily consistent with your desired future. In other words, the people and things you allow to influence your thinking can have an overwhelming affect on your performance and whether you succeed or fail in life. Proactively guarding information inflow from the various media available could be called *new age responsibility*. While it's a good thing to have access to information, if we don't keenly control what's coming at us, when it's getting to us, and how it's getting to us, it can easily become information overload. While there have been many studies that suggest that we have the mental capacity to consume massive amounts of information, uncontrolled information can lead to chaos and confusion. This is especially the case when that information is sent from sources that have specific intent to influence and sometimes manipulate.

Freedom of Speech

In the United States, the First Amendment gives us all the right to freedom of speech. With the exception of a few rules and regulations intended to maintain civility and order, we can say what we want to say. This is really an awesome thing, and it is one of the basic rights that make being a US citizen a worthwhile ambition of many people around the world. However, with such a powerful freedom or basic right, comes massive individual responsibility. We are individually responsible for consciously controlling and organizing the information available to us. Basically, we are all responsible for creating our own filters.

Creating Filters

As I mentioned earlier, the information superhighway has ushered in a whole new world of information availability. In addition to the printed forms of media and content that were available to us in the past, we can now learn or find information about anything we want to know using a computer or one of the numerous PDAs or smartphones on the market today. It's all at our fingertips. Until the last twenty years, this sort of information has never been available to the majority of humankind. That's a phenomena of recent history that we tend to forget as time passes and we continue to infuse even newer technologies that deliver such massive amounts of information. And this explosion of information has become one of the greatest social, economical, and political equalizers.

Take Action Now!

This books was meant to be short. Sitting down and doing the exercises is what will really make a difference in your life. Please don't get caught up with the concepts, ideas and theories I've presented here and just make sure you do the recommended exercises. Don't let anything get in the way of doing what matters most. It's essential that you spend time pondering your future and making sure your goals and dreams are in line with your purpose in life. Mind mapping or drawing it out should be a helpful exercise but don't even let that get in your way. Write it out, draw it, record it or even use video to crystallize the things you would like to accomplish. It is not a myth that the vast majority of people do not write down their goals. Decide that you have a High Octane Performance engine and determine to live the rest of your life maintaining it.

RECOMMENDED RESOURCES

The following is a list of resources pertaining to the concepts discussed in this book.

Please keep in mind; however, that the most effective thing you can do is grab a piece a paper and start writing or drawing out each of your wheels. Doing so is the crucial starting point to gaining clarity on what's important to you, and will give you greater insight into your mission. If you get stuck, reaching out to someone who understands the HOP method is the ideal way to complete your exercises.

Determining your mission
- http://www.highoctaneperformance.com/defining-your-mission

Developing your financial wheel
- http://www.highoctaneperformance.com/your-financial-wheel

Developing your education wheel
- http://www.highoctaneperformance.com/your-educational-wheel

Developing your relationship wheel
- http://www.highoctaneperformance.com/your-relationship-wheel

Developing your steering wheel
- http://www.highoctaneperformance.com/creating-your-wheels-mind-mapping

Take the Thirty-Day Success Challenge
- http://www.30daysuccesschallenge.com/

Finding a HOP coach
- http://hopcoaching.com/

Videos that feed your spirit and help you burn 93 octane
- http://www.highoctaneperformance.com/gas-the-secret-formula-committing-to-spiritual-strength

Start building your support group, mastermind, or steering committee
- http://HOPcommunity.com

ABOUT THE AUTHOR

Clarence Williams has spent most of his professional career in business consulting, information technology, sales and business development. Working with and coaching individuals who have a burning desire to succeed is his vocation. Like many of the individuals he's had an opportunity to coach, everyday is a continuous effort to contribute to society and be among the talented tenth.

www.ingramcontent.com/pod-product-compliance
Lightning Source LLC
Chambersburg PA
CBHW071852020426
42331CB00007B/1964